DAILY LIFE IN ANCIENT INDIA

LEEANN BLANKENSHIP

ROSEN
PUBLISHING®

New York

Published in 2017 by The Rosen Publishing Group, Inc.
29 East 21st Street, New York, NY 10010

Copyright © 2017 by The Rosen Publishing Group, Inc.

First Edition

Library of Congress Cataloging-in-Publication Data

Names: Blankenship, LeeAnn, author.
Title: Daily life in ancient India / LeeAnn Blankenship.
Description: First edition. | New York : Rosen Publishing, 2017. | Series: Spotlight on the rise and fall of ancient civilizations | Includes bibliographical references and index. | Audience: Grades 7-12.
Identifiers: LCCN 2016000819| ISBN 9781477789520 (library bound) | ISBN 9781477789162 (pbk.) | ISBN 9781477789179 (6-pack)
Subjects: LCSH: India--Social life and customs--To 1200. | India--History--Maurya dynasty, ca. 322 B.C.-ca. 185 B.C. | Gupta dynasty. | India--History--Gupta dynasty
Classification: LCC DS425 .B63 2016 | DDC 934/.01--dc23
LC record available at http://lccn.loc.gov/2016000819

Manufactured in the United States of America

CONTENTS

INDIA'S FIRST CIVILIZATIONS

Over four thousand years ago, farmers in ancient India learned to grow surplus food. That meant others were free to develop skills like brickmaking and woodworking. People began to trade what they produced.

Soon they built permanent villages, then towns and cities. Eventually three ancient civilizations developed.

Each had a central government to make rules and keep order. The earliest civilization was the Indus Valley, followed by the Maurya and the Gupta.

The Indus Valley civilization is the most mysterious. It developed near the Indus and Saraswati Rivers. It covered most of what is now Pakistan and northwest India, as well as part of Afghanistan. Discovered less than a century ago, its ruins still hold many secrets.

The Indus people had a written language, but modern day scholars are unable to decipher it. Most likely, it would reveal many details about life back then. For now, however, all we can do is study the fascinating objects its people left behind.

The Indus Valley civilization developed around fertile river valleys that provided rich agricultural lands for the Indus people.

FAMILY LIFE IN THE INDUS VALLEY (2600–1900 BCE)

Most Indus people farmed in the country. Others were fishermen, herders, miners, and traders. In the cities, some men were laborers or specialized in metal, shell, or stonework. Others made jewelry, seals, or bricks. Some were ivory carvers, potters, and carpenters. No doubt, there were merchants, religious leaders, and rulers.

Some families were wealthier than others, but almost everyone had adequate food and comfortable housing.

The fathers were the heads of their families. Mothers were probably in charge of the household responsibilities and children. They cooked food and used spinning wheels and looms to make cloth.

Most likely, children helped with chores. They enjoyed board games, toys, and music. Family pets were sometimes dogs, cats, or even monkeys. Learning was important. Children were taught at home by the oldest male in the family, usually their father.

Some Indus families may have had servants. And everyone appears to have enjoyed something special—peace. There is little evidence of crime, fighting, or war.

Those who supplied food were the backbone of Indus civilization. This carving from one of the cave temples of Mahabalipuram illustrates that cows and cattle have always been greatly valued by Indian society.

INDUS VALLEY HOUSES

The Indus civilization was dependent on its farmers. They, in turn, were supported by herdsmen and hunter-gatherers. These groups lived in rural areas. Hunter-gatherers and herdsmen had seasonal camps. Farmers lived in villages, probably in circular huts with rammed-earth floors. Their dwellings were built of wooden posts with wattle and daub.

In cities, most homes were constructed with uniform, baked mud bricks. One- to three-stories tall, they had flat roofs and windows with wooden lattice. Walls were plastered and no doubt painted with colorful designs. Families could enjoy shade and fresh air in each home's central courtyard. Rooms off the courtyard included a small kitchen with a hearth. Stairs led to the upper levels.

Many houses had a private well. Others got water from one of many public reservoirs or cisterns. Remarkably, most homes had a bathroom with a shower and toilet. A system of drains connected to a citywide sanitation system was thousands of years ahead of its time.

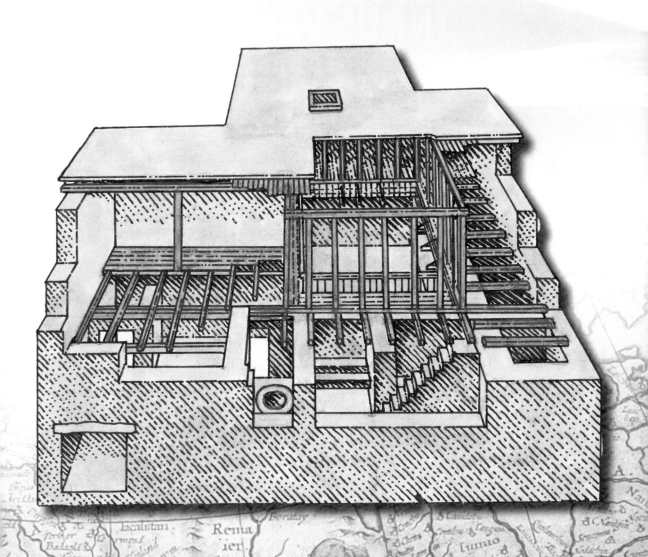

This drawing shows a large house, probably for a well-to-do family in the Indus Valley city of Mohenjo-Daro. It had a bathroom and sewer system for removal of waste water.

FOOD IN THE INDUS VALLEY

Indus Valley people ate a varied, well-balanced diet. Farmers cultivated wheat, barley, and pulses. They grew vegetables and fruits such as dates, grapes, melons, and jujubes. Hunter-gatherers probably supplied foods like honey, nuts, and berries.

Cattle, pigs, sheep, and goats were used for meat and dairy. By this time, chickens had been domesticated from the jungle and were used for meat and eggs. Meat was also available by hunting and included deer and antelope, wild pigs, lizards, and waterfowl such as ducks.

Ancient paintings and pottery show that people fished with nets weighted down with net-sinkers. They also used hooks and lines. Many copper fishhooks have been found all over the civilization, showing us that fishing was common. Dried salt-water fish were transported inland from the coast. People caught fresh fish like catfish and carp locally.

Around 2000 BCE, rice and millet began to be grown in some areas. Their cultivation was of vital importance to the success of the Indus Valley civilization.

Hunters supplemented the Indus diet by harvesting wild birds such as jungle fowl. Their eggs, as well as their meat, added to the variety of Indus meals.

INDUS VALLEY CLOTHING AND JEWELRY

Most Indus Valley clothing was cotton. Women wore short knee-length skirts and a beaded belt of many strands. Men's garments were drawn up between the legs and tucked in at the back. Men may have worn turbans. Priests or rulers might have had robes draped over one shoulder.

Hairstyles and jewelry probably indicated status. Sometimes men and women wore a straight fillet tied with a cord around their foreheads.

They liked bangles and wore them more than people of any other ancient civilization. At the wrist, bangles were narrow; above the elbow, they were wider. Many were terra-cotta or shell. Wealthier people chose copper, bronze, gold, and faience.

Women wore finger and toe rings of silver and copper wire. Long cone-shaped amulets around their necks may have indicated marital status. Multiple strands of beaded necklaces covered almost their entire chest.

Men probably wore hair ornaments with tiny beads. They shaved their upper lip but had short beards.

Figurines like this one found in Mohenjo-Daro indicate that women of the Indus Valley wore short skirts, many strands of beads, and a complex arrangement of hair, flowers, or other ornaments on their heads.

RELIGION IN THE INDUS VALLEY

We know little about Indus Valley religion, but many of their artifacts seem connected to religion.

A stone bust from Mohenjo-Daro is called the "Priest-King." It has features suggesting the man may depict a god or a ruler approved by the gods.

Some clay figurines are described as mother goddesses. They could have been used in fertility ceremonies. Male figurines with horned headdresses might represent gods.

It is believed that the pipal (fig) tree with its heart-shaped leaves was worshiped. Scenes on pottery, paintings, and seals imply exactly that.

We know from our study of Indus ruins that people were very concerned about cleanliness. This was so extreme it indicates ritual religious bathing. There are also shrines in homes and fire altars at many sites.

Even burial sites give us clues. They often include bones of animals used as sacrifices. Objects buried with the dead suggest a belief in life after death.

The "Priest-King" sculpture wears a headband with a round ornament and a similar, smaller ornament on his upper arm. A cloak on his left shoulder may indicate his status.

THE RISE OF THE MAURYAN EMPIRE (321–185 BCE)

After the Indus Valley civilization declined, independent kingdom-states eventually arose. In 321 BCE, warrior-king Chandragupta Maurya seized the most powerful kingdom. He established the Maurya Empire. It had three notable kings: Chandragupta, followed by his son Bindusara, and then Bindusara's son, Ashoka.

Each was head of a strong central government with a vast network of spies and secret police. The empire was divided into provinces with special officers to govern.

The king's luxurious palace was in the capital city, Pataliputra. His army included over half a million soldiers. There were also ten thousand horse-drawn chariots and nine thousand war elephants.

A strict tax system as well as tributes funded the government. Standard weights and measures ensured honesty. People used a single currency throughout the empire. Trade flourished.

The king sought to control crime, protect his subjects, and keep peace. His public projects built canals, wells, and reservoirs. People enjoyed free hospital care and well-maintained roads with rest houses.

At its height, the Mauryan Empire was one of the largest empires of the world.

MAURYAN FAMILY LIFE

In Mauryan society, joint families were common. Several generations lived in one house with a single kitchen. They ate together and shared religious beliefs and financial assets.

Families were patriarchal, with the oldest male at the head. His word was the final authority.

Marriage was important. Only royalty or the wealthy were allowed more than one wife. Occasionally, a man took a second wife if his first had no children or only daughters. Divorce was allowed if both parties agreed or if one abandoned the other. In such cases, women often kept the property that had been given to them as a bride gift.

Women were excluded from politics, but crimes against them were severely punished. Most worked in the home. A few became temple dancers or court attendants. Some were even spies or bodyguards for the king. But poor women and widows sometimes worked for government officers by spinning or weaving or in agricultural jobs.

This Ajanta Cave painting gives us a glimpse into the skills of people who lived in ancient India.

FOOD IN MAURYAN TIMES

Mauryans enjoyed many of the same foods and cooking styles their ancestors had. There were new varieties of rice and barley. More people ate wheat and pulses, and soups were popular.

Food choices depended mostly on two seasons. In the winter, rice and millet grew. Wheat and barley were the primary summer crops. The people also ate other cereals and dairy products from cows, water buffalo, sheep, and goats.

Many diets included meat, fish, and chicken. Some Mauryans became vegetarians as Buddhism grew in popularity.

Some recipes used spices like salt, long pepper, ginger, cloves, coriander, turmeric, cumin, and cardamom. Sugar cane grew wild and was used along with honey to sweeten foods.

Grapes, dates, jujubes, and melons were still enjoyed, and bananas had been introduced. It is possible that Indian food scientists bred the pomelo and mandarin to produce bitter and sweet oranges. Wine and rice beer were common along with buttermilk, fruit juice, and liquors.

This frieze from the Stupa of Sanchi depicts life during the Mauryan dynasty. Rice, millet, and barley were staples of their diet.

MAURYAN EDUCATION

Young Mauryans were usually schooled at home by an older male relative. Much learning was based on religious books called the Vedas. Among their studies were grammar, composition, multiplication tables, and recitation of hymns and incantations. In addition, girls learned domestic skills.

A boy's higher education began when he was about fourteen. Under the Hindu Gurukul system, he went to live with or near a teacher. Some went to Buddhist monasteries instead. Such opportunities were rarely available for girls.

Teachers or gurus were held in high esteem. Education was free, available to even the poorest of students. Teachers were paid by voluntary gifts from more prosperous families.

Students did household chores or farm work for their teacher. Their day began early. To develop character, food and clothing were simple but sufficient. Since books were costly and rare, students trained themselves to remember everything discussed. Subjects included the Vedas, philosophy, classical literature, grammar and law.

This painting depicts the god Brahma offering a page of the Vedas, or Hindu Scriptures, to a follower. Brahma is said to be the creator of knowledge and the universe.

MAURYAN CLOTHING

Mauryan men and women, especially those in urban areas, wore three primary unstitched garments.

The main garment was the *antariya*. It was a length of white cotton or linen draped around the hips and pulled up between the legs. Sometimes women wore it like a skirt. At the waist, a sash called a *kayabandh* was tied to secure the antariya.

The *uttariya* was another long cloth draped over the top part of the body. It was worn over one or both shoulders, diagonally across the chest, or even loosely across the back. Among upper class women, it was often decorated and used as a head covering. For the laborer, it could be tied around the head to protect him from the sun or used to wipe sweat off his face.

Some Mauryan people still lived in remote areas and wore simple garments of coarse cotton. More primitive forest dwellers dressed in skins, furs, and clothes made from grasses.

This terra-cotta figure from the Mauryan period shows the antariya worn as a skirt. An uttariya covers the head.

RELIGION IN THE MAURYAN EMPIRE

Mauryans practiced Hinduism, Buddhism, or Jainism. Most were Hindu with altars in their homes for worship. Hinduism developed from the Vedas and other writings in about 1500 BCE. Hindus worshiped many gods, which they saw as expressions of one supreme being. They believed in reincarnation and karma. Hinduism promoted the caste system.

Buddhist philosophy taught people to look within themselves for truth. Buddhists also believed in karma and sought spiritual peace called nirvana.

Around 262 BCE, Mauryan king Ashoka invaded a neighboring republic. The war's brutality was so disturbing, he gradually converted to Buddhism.

Throughout India, Ashoka erected stone pillars with edicts urging his people to be just and compassionate. He built thousands of Buddhist shrines called stupas.

Jainism shared some Hindu beliefs but rejected the caste system. Like Buddhists, Jains searched within for truth, strove to rid themselves of earthly desires, and loved all living creatures.

The Dhamekh Stupa (500 BCE) replaced an earlier structure Ashoka built in 249 BCE. It is said to mark the place where Buddha gave his first sermon after his enlightenment.

THE GUPTA EMPIRE (319–540 CE)

In 185 BCE, the Mauryan king was assassinated and the empire collapsed. For about five hundred years, no unifying government ruled. Then the Gupta dynasty came to power. Except for their names, we have little information about the first two kings. But some later history was recorded in inscriptions and other written records. We know the third ruler was Chandragupta I. His reign began about 319 CE.

Over the course of the next 220 years, there were various Gupta rulers. The son of Chandragupta I, Samudragupta, greatly expanded the empire's area. Samudragupta's son, Chandragupta II, enlarged it even more. The most successful and culturally rich Gupta era was during his reign.

The Gupta kings used lofty titles, but they actually had less control over their empire than the Mauryans had. Their dynasty benefitted the upper castes more than the lower. Nevertheless, it did support the sciences, art, and literature. It is called the "Golden Age" of India.

Castes are illustrated here with the highest caste, Brahman (priest), in the center back. Below him in descending order are the Kashatriya (warrior), Vaishya (trader), and Sudra (worker).

FAMILY LIFE IN THE GUPTA EMPIRE

Poor villagers lived in simple houses, often in joint families. Young boys herded cattle with their fathers or worked in the fields. Girls helped at home. Other joint families, especially city dwellers, lived in better houses. All were under the authority of the male family head.

In wealthier families, young children were undisciplined and enjoyed life. Both husbands and wives performed daily rites. A domestic fire was tended so it never went out. Twice a day, the family gathered at the fire's altar for offerings before meals.

During this time, the status of women became more restricted. The wife treated her husband as master. She dealt with household affairs and rarely left home. When she did, she was always chaperoned.

Polygamy was allowed. It occurred more among the upper caste *kshatriyas*. There were several kinds of marriages, and people usually married within their caste. Girls sometimes became brides before adolescence. A widower was expected to marry again right away. Remarriage for widows was frowned upon.

This princely couple from a painting in Ajanta Cave 17 illustrates the importance of marriage and family life in Gupta society.

FOOD IN THE GUPTA EMPIRE

Rice was at the heart of many Gupta diets. Mixed with clarified butter, curd, or molasses, it made a tasty gruel. It could be a main dish or made into flour for flatbread pancakes.

People ate soups as well as wheat, barley, chickpeas, beans, and lentils. Many dairy products were popular.

Because of Buddhism and Jainism beliefs, vegetarianism increased. Leafy greens and vegetables like gourds and pumpkins were popular. Mushrooms, sprouts, garlic, and onions were prohibited. Some people still ate meat and fish. Goat, sheep, and beef were delicacies, but chicken and eggs of any kind were less desirable. Crocodile, porpoise, and some birds were taboo.

Many spices, oils, honey, and sugarcane continued in use. As in the past, fruits included grapes, dates, jujubes, oranges, melons, and bananas. People also enjoyed pomegranates, mangoes, pears, lemons, plums, peaches, and apricots.

They drank water, milk, whey, fruit juices, and wine. A variety of intoxicating drinks were popular with women, especially royalty.

Trade and farming flourished across the Gupta Empire. Assorted varieties of rice were developed, no doubt similar to these at a modern-day Indian market.

EDUCATION IN THE GUPTA EMPIRE

Many villagers farmed like their parents. Others learned a profession by becoming an apprentice. For the rest, Gupta education was similar to Mauryan.

Early schooling began at home. For children in wealthier families, it might continue there. Others, however, learned from a local teacher. Classes were held outside under trees in the central courtyard.

Most ancient education was verbal. Books were costly and rare. Students practiced writing in the sand with sticks. Sometimes they wrote on a board. Much of their schooling was lectures, discussions, and recitation.

At about age eight, boys could begin a more formal Hindu or Buddhist education. Both required students to leave home to live with their Hindu guru or in a Buddhist ashram or monastery. Opportunities for women were very limited with stricter rules.

During the Gupta period, several universities offered advanced education. Taxila was the most important. It attracted scholars from India as well as hundreds from foreign countries.

Taxila was considered to be one of the earliest universities in the world. Its ruins near the city of Rawalpindi, Pakistan, have been designated as a UNESCO World Heritage Site.

GUPTA CLOTHING

In Gupta times, people wore traditional clothing, but stitched garments (like coats and trousers) gained favor. Turbans were mainly worn by officials.

Styles for the antariya varied. Many women wrapped and tucked it in at the left hip under their navel. This *lehnga* style was thought more feminine than pulling it between one's legs.

A *bhairnivasani* was a gathered skirt held by a girdle. Some village women wore a narrow drawstring skirt called a *ghagri*. It had a flattering vertical border in the front.

Women began to clothe the tops of their bodies with a *choli*. This short-sleeved, low-necked garment was cropped so the wearer's navel showed. The uttariya became sheer.

Men and women liked jewelry, especially gold. The *vijayantika* was a desirable necklace of pearls, rubies, emeralds, sapphires, and diamonds. Earrings, arm ornaments, anklets, bracelets, and rings were popular. Flowers were fashionable both on the body and in the hair. Kings even wore white flowers on military trips.

This sculpture depicts the Hindu god Shiva wearing an abundance of ornamental jewelry, much like that worn by Gupta women.

RELIGION IN GUPTA TIMES

Gupta society was built on a Hindu structure. Its caste system decided a person's worth and life role. This was true regardless of religious beliefs.

Most Indian people had begun speaking Sanskrit, the language of the ancient texts. It was even used in literature, government, business, and science.

Rituals and sacrifice were the main ways people expressed their Hindu faith. There were also many festivals. Pilgrimages to holy sites became more important. So did bathing in sacred rivers.

The popularity of Buddhism declined. Buddhist dislike of the caste system presented big problems. To most Hindus, it challenged the whole structure of their world. It also meant a threat to deeply held doctrines.

The Gupta kings were Hindu. That strengthened the position of Hinduism in the empire. But they also were tolerant of other religions and supported non-Hindu art and literature.

This period also saw the beginnings of Sakti cults based on indigenous beliefs.

This stone relief from a Vishnu temple located in Deogarh, India, was built in the late Gupta period (c. 500 CE). It is one of the earliest surviving temples and an excellent example of Gupta architecture.

HOW THE PAST AFFECTS THE PRESENT

None of these ancient civilizations still exist. But today, many elements of each are reflected in the everyday lives of the Indian people.

Just as it was in the Indus Valley thousands of years ago, the family continues to be of vital importance. Today, several generations still live under the same roof in joint family arrangements.

The influence of ancient religions is easy to spot in the country's many temples, mosques, and gurdwaras. Glimpses of the ancient styles of traditional dress can still be seen in some of today's fashions. Many of the same foods are cooked and enjoyed at mealtimes. Though Sanskrit is primarily used only by modern-day Hindu priests during religious ceremonies, it is still one of India's twenty-two scheduled languages.

The people of any civilization are really its heart. Though people and their world may pass away, the echoes of their legacies continue from generation to generation.

Just as their ancestors may have, this royal family is observing Holi, an ancient two-day Hindu celebration of spring that is called the Festival of Colours.

GLOSSARY

caste system A rigid structure that divides people into hereditary classes, restricting their professions as well as their associations.

cistern An underground tank for storing rainwater.

civilization A large group of culturally similar people who share advances in the way they are governed, how work is divided, and how food is grown; often characterized by improvements in science and technology and a written language.

faience Glazed ceramics (usually blue, green, or chocolate-red in color) made from crushed quartz or sand crystals.

hunter-gatherer A person from a nomadic group that lives by hunting and gathering wild foods and animals.

jujube A wrinkled fruit similar to an apple in firmness and taste with a single pit at its center; a Chinese date.

karma The belief that a person's actions, either good or bad, bring similar results to his or her present or future life.

mandarin A small orange that grew wild in India thousands of years ago.

millet A grass grown for its small grain.

patriarchal A system where men have authority over women and property is inherited through the male family line.

polygamy The practice of being married to more than one person at a time, especially a wife.

reincarnation The belief that when a person dies, his or her soul will come back to earth in another body or form.

seal A carved soapstone square used to make an imprint in wax or clay to claim an object, sign a document, or mark a package.

wattle and daub A way of building walls by interweaving sticks and twigs and covering them with mud, clay, and sand mixed with straw.

Amnesty International India
4th Floor, Statesman House
Connaught Place
New Delhi, Delhi
India 110001
Website: http://www.amnesty.org.in
Amnesty International India is a global movement involved in protect-
ing people who are denied justice or freedom in India.

Anthropological Survey of India
27 Jawaharlal Nehru Road
Kolkata, West Bengal
India 700016
Website: http://www.ansi.gov.in
The ANSI pursues anthropological research and projects through the
government of India.

Embassy of India
2107 Massachusetts Avenue NW
Washington, DC 20008
(202) 939-7000
Website: http://www.indianembassy.org
The Indian embassy represents the country of India in the United States.

Indian Council for Cultural Relations (ICCR)
Azad Bhavan
I.P. Estate
New Delhi, Delhi
India 110002

Website: http://www.iccr.gov.in
The Indian Council for Cultural Relations forms and implements policies and programs pertaining to India's external cultural relations with other countries

Wildlife Protection Society of India
S-25 Panchpark
New Delhi, Delhi
India 110017
Website: http://www.wpsi-india.org
This nonprofit organization focuses on the conservation of tigers, elephants, leopards, and other wild species in India through wildlife enforcement to end poaching and illegal wildlife trade in India.

WEBSITES

Because of the changing nature of Internet links, Rosen Publishing has developed an online list of websites related to the subject of this book. This site is updated regularly. Please use this link to access the list:

http://www.rosenlinks.com/SRFAC/idaily

FOR FURTHER READING

Ali, Daud. *Hands on History! Ancient India.* Wigston, Leicestershire, England: Anness Publishing, 2013.

Bankston, John. *Ancient India, Maurya Empire*. Hockessin, DE: Mitchell Lane Publishers, 2013.

Fullman, Joseph. *Ancient Civilizations*. New York, NY: Dorling Kindersley, 2013.

Holm, Kirsten. *Everyday Life in Ancient India*. New York, NY: Rosen Publishing Group, 2012.

Laser, Tammy, ed. *Gods and Goddesses of Ancient India*. New York, NY: Britannica Educational Publishing, 2015.

Lassieur, Allison. *Ancient India*. Jefferson City, MO: Scholastic Library Publishing, 2012.

Nardo, Don. *India*. New York, NY: Children's Press, 2012.

Quick, P. S. *The Incredible Indus Valley*. Luton, England: Andrews UK Limited, 2015.

Rowell, Rebecca. *Ancient India*. Minneapolis, MN: Abdo Publishing, 2015.

Williams, Brian. *Daily Life in the Indus Valley Civilization*. Portsmouth, NH: Heinemann Publishing, 2015.

Williams, Marcia. *The Elephant's Friend and Other Tales from Ancient India*. Cambridge, MA: Candlewick, 2012.

BIBLIOGRAPHY

Ahmed, Mukhtar. *Ancient Pakistan, An Archaeological History. Volume III—Harappan Civilization—The Material Culture*. Reidsville, NC: Foursome Group, 2014.

Coningham, Robin, and Ruth Young, eds. *The Archaeology of South Asia, from the Indus to Asoka, c. 6500-200 CE*. New York, NY: Cambridge University Press, 2015.

Deka, B. *Higher Education in India, Development and Problems*. New Delhi, India: Atlantic Publishers & Distributors, 2000.

Hyslop, Steven G., and Patricia Daniels. *Great Empires, An Illustrated Atlas*. Washington, DC: National Geographic, 2012.

Kaushik, Roy. *Hinduism and the Ethics of Warfare in South Asia from Antiquity to the Present*. Cambridge, England: Cambridge University Press, 2012.

Keay, John. *India, A History*. New York, NY: Atlantic Monthly Press, 2000.

Kenoyer, Jonathan Mark. *Ancient Cities of the Indus Valley Civilization*. Oxford, England: Oxford University Press, 1998.

Kulke, Hermann, and Dietmar Rothermund. *A History of India (Fifth Edition)*. London and New York: Routledge, 2010.

Lowenstein, Tom. *The Civilization of Ancient India and Southeast Asia*. New York, NY: Rosen Publishing, 2013.

McIntosh, Jane. *A Peaceful Realm, The Rise and Fall of the Indus Civilization*. New York, NY: Nevraumont Publishing, 2002.

McLeod, John. *The History of India*. Santa Barbara, CA: Greenwood, 2015.

Olson, Carl. *The Many Colors of Hinduism, A Thematic-Historical Introduction*. New Brunswick, NJ: Rutgers University Press, 2007.

Sen, Sailendra Nath. *Ancient Indian History and Civilization*. New Delhi, India: New Age International Limited Publishers, 1988.

Sharma, R. S. *India's Ancient Past*. New Delhi, India: Oxford University Press, 2005.

INDEX

ABOUT THE AUTHOR

Every Saturday morning growing up in the 1950s, LeeAnn Blankenship watched *Andy's Gang* on her family's black-and-white TV. It featured a series she loved, which was set in the jungles of India. LeeAnn was captivated by the mysterious land and the unique flora and fauna depicted on-screen.

Now a retired teacher and social worker, LeeAnn enjoys writing for children. When she had the opportunity to write about ancient India, she jumped at the chance.

LeeAnn has published numerous magazine articles, poetry, and one children's picture book.

PHOTO CREDITS

Cover, p. 1 Frank Bienewald/LightRocketGetty Images, p. 3 Alexander Mazurkevich/Shutterstock.com; pp. 5, 9, 17, 29 Dorling Kindersley/Getty Images; p. 7 uniquely india/Getty Images; p 11 Universal Images Group/Getty Images; p. 13 DEA/G. Nimatallah/De Agostini/Getty Images; p. 15 DEA/A. Dagli Orti/De Agostini/Getty Images; p. 19 Borromeo/Art Resource, NY; p. 21 © imageBROKER/Alamy Stock Photo; p. 23 India Office Library, London/Ann & Bury Peerless Picture Library/Bridgeman Images; p. 25 © ephotocorp/Alamy Stock Photo; p. 27 IndiaPictures/Universal Images Group/Getty Images; pp. 31, 39 Bridgeman Images; p. 33 PhotoAlto/Isabelle Rozenbaum/Getty Images; p. 35 Photo © Luca Tettoni/Bridgeman Images; p. 37 © Haydn Hansell/Alamy Stock Photo; p. 41 Martin Harvey/Photolibrary/Getty Images; cover, p. 1 floral graphic Shymko Svitlana/Shutterstock.com; back cover and interior pages background map Marzolino/Shutterstock.com; cover and interior pages background textures and patterns zffoto/Shutterstock.com, Elena Larina/Shutterstock.com, Ilaszlo/Shutterstock.com

Designer: Michael Moy; Editor: Christine Poolos; Photo Researcher: Nicole Baker